This book belongs to:

_____

to:
Harmony
Kensley
Gianna
Cassius
Dallas
Josiah
Elijah
Penelope

Jesus loves you, and so do I.

God's Word Is Like...
Word Pictures that Bring the Bible to Life

Copyright 2024 by Akaya Kitchen. All rights reserved.

All Bible quotations within are from the World English Bible British Edition.

The Book of Books reproduced with permission from Emmaus Worldwide, copyright 1933. Written by Alfred P. Gibbs.

Cover design by Akaya Kitchen
Interior designs by Akaya Kitchen

ISBN: 9780997815870

Published by Akaya Kitchen

Printed in the United States of America

God's Word Is Like...

Word Pictures that Bring the Bible to Life

Akaya Kitchen

God's Word is like a light.
It helps me see where I should go.

Your word is a lamp to my feet, and a light for my path.
Psalm 119:105

God's Word is like a hiding place.
It keeps me safe from trouble.

You are my hiding place and my shield. I hope in your word.
Psalm 119:114

God's Word is like a seed.
It grows when planted in my heart.

Having been born again, not of corruptible seed, but of incorruptible, through the word of God, which lives and remains forever.
1 Peter 1:23

God's Word is like a map.

It shows me the way I should go.

Guide me in your truth, and teach me,
For you are the God of my salvation. I wait for you all day long.
Psalm 25:5

God's Word is like water.
It washes me and makes me clean.

That he might sanctify her, having cleansed her by the washing of water with the word, that he might present the assembly to himself gloriously, not having spot or wrinkle or any such thing, but that she should be holy and without defect.
Ephesians 5:26-27

God's Word is like honey.

It is sweet and yummy to my taste.

**How sweet are your promises to my taste,
more than honey to my mouth!
Psalm 119:103**

God's Word is like an umbrella.
It protects me from the storms.

Everyone therefore who hears these words of mine and does them, I will liken him to a wise man who built his house on a rock. The rain came down, the floods came, and the winds blew and beat on that house; and it didn't fall, for it was founded on the rock.

Matthew 7:24-25

God's Word is like gold and silver.
It is valuable to me.

The law of your mouth is better to me than thousands of pieces of gold and silver.
Psalm 119:72

God's Word is like a hammer.
It breaks hard things into pieces.

"Isn't my word like fire?" says the LORD;
"and like a hammer that breaks the rock in pieces?"
Jeremiah 23:29

God's Word is like medicine.
It makes me well when I am sick.

**My son, attend to my words...For they are life
to those who find them, and health to their whole body.
Proverbs 4:20-22**

God's Word is like a hug.
It comforts me when I am sad.

This is my comfort in my affliction, for your word has revived me.
Psalm 119:50

God's Word is like a fire.
It burns within our hearts.

They said to one another, "Weren't our hearts burning within us while he spoke to us along the way, and while he opened the Scriptures to us?"
Luke 24:32

God's Word is like a letter.
It is a message to me from God.

It shall be with him, and he shall read from it all the days of his life, that he may learn to fear the LORD his God, to keep all the words of this law and these statutes, to do them.

Deuteronomy 17:19

God's Word is like a teacher.
It tells me what I need to know.

Every Scripture is God-breathed and profitable for teaching, for reproof, for correction, and for instruction in righteousness.
2 Timothy 3:16

God's Word is like a whisper.
I have to listen closely to hear it.

...After the wind there was an earthquake; but the LORD was not in the earthquake. After the earthquake a fire passed; but the LORD was not in the fire. After the fire, there was a still small voice.
1 Kings 19:11-12

God's Word is like a mirror.
It shows me how I look.

For if anyone is a hearer of the word and not a doer, he is like a man looking at his natural face in a mirror; for he sees himself, and goes away, and immediately forgets what kind of man he was. But he who looks into the perfect law of freedom and continues, not being a hearer who forgets but a doer of the work, this man will be blessed in what he does.

James 1:23-25

God's Word is like a sword.
With it, I defeat the enemy.

And take the helmet of salvation, and the sword of the Spirit, which is the word of God.

Ephesians 6:17

God's Word is greater than all things.
It will last forever.

Heaven and earth will pass away, but my words will not pass away.
Matthew 24:35

The Gospel

In the beginning, God created people in order to have a relationship with them. Sadly, people turned against God in sin, and sin separated people from Him. But God had a plan to save them from their sins.

He chose a man named Abraham to carry his promises, and God promised that He would bless all the people of the earth through Abraham's family. In the Bible, we read that God passed those promises down to Abraham's family, the Israelites, also known as the Jews. God promised that he would send an Anointed One to Israel to save the Israelites and the people of the entire world from their sins.

One day, God sent the Anointed One, His Son, Jesus (in Hebrew, His name is Yeshua), and he died for Israel's sins and for the sins of the whole world. Three days later, God raised Him from the dead, and now He is seated in heaven at the right hand of God the Father.

People from all nations everywhere are invited to put their trust in Jesus to be saved from their sins. You can also put your trust in Jesus and follow His way of living. If you put your trust in Jesus, you can say a prayer like this one:

A Prayer for Salvation

God, thank you for sending Jesus to save me from my sins. Forgive me for the things I have done wrong, and help me to live for You. Come to live in my heart and show me how to follow You.
In Jesus' Name, Amen.

A Prayer for the Salvation of Israel (the Jewish People)

After Jesus rose from the dead and ascended to heaven, many Jews trusted Jesus, but sadly, most of them did not. The Bible says that one day, all of the Jews will be saved. Would you pray for the salvation of the Jewish people?

God, I pray for the Jewish people and ask
You to bring them to salvation.
In Jesus' Name, Amen.

"Brothers, my heart's desire and my prayer to God is for Israel, that they may be saved."
Romans 10:1

The God's Word...
Children's Book Series

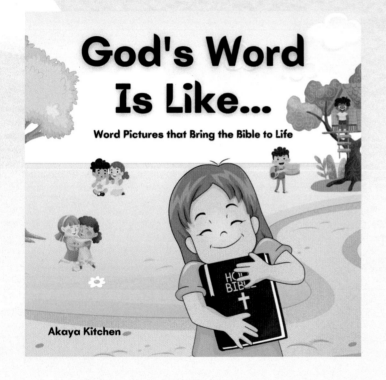

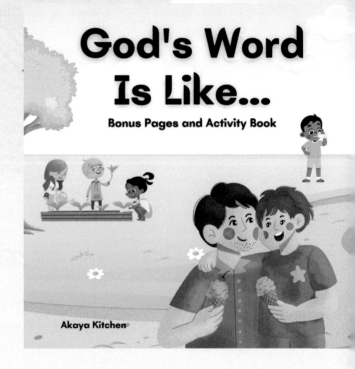

www.akayakitchen.com

For every book sold, a donation is made to Lifting up Zion.

www.liftingupzion.org

The Book of Books

God's Word is like a hammer
That breaketh the rock in twain;
A lamp to guide our footsteps,
And a light on the stormy main;
A sword that has two edges,
And a mirror ourselves to see.
Oh, yes, this is the best of books,
The B-I-B-L-E.

God's Word is like a lighthouse,
On a wild and stormy sea.
It points to Christ, the Savior,
Bidding us from wrath to flee.
He wrote it by His Spirit,
It was given for you and me.
Oh, yes, this is the best of books,
The B-I-B-L-E.

'Tis living seed that groweth
When into the heart received.
Like milk and meat will cause to grow
All those who on Christ believe.
Like water it will cleanse us,
From defilement will set us free.
O yes this is the Book of books,
The B-I-B-L-E.

- Alfred P. Gibbs
1933
Printed with permission

Made in the USA
Monee, IL
15 December 2024